My Journey To HEALING

Bev Weirather

Copyright © 2013 by Bev Weirather

All rights reserved. No part of this book may be used, reproduced, stored in a retrieval system, or transmitted in any form whatsoever — including electronic, photocopy, recording — without prior written permission from the author, except in the case of brief quotations embodied in critical articles or reviews.

Scripture quotations are taken from the *Holy Bible, New King James Version*, Copyright © 1982 by Thomas Nelson, Inc.

The *Amplified® Bible*, Copyright © 1954, 1958, 1962, 1964, 1965, 1987 by The Lockman Foundation. Used by permission." (www.Lockman.org)

The Holy Bible, New International Version®. NIV®. Copyright © 1973, 1978, 1984 by International Bible Society. Used by permission of Zondervan. All rights reserved.

The Holy Bible, English Standard Version ®. Copyright© 2001 by Crossway Bibles, a publishing ministry of Good News Publishers. Used by permission. All rights reserved.

FIRST EDITION

ISBN: 978-1-939748-28-7

Library of Congress Control Number: 2013950057

Published by
NewBookPublishing.com, a division of Reliance Media, Inc.
515 Cooper Commerce Drive, #140, Apopka, FL 32703
NewBookPublishing.com

Printed in the United States of America

Disclaimer: The views and opinions expressed in this book are solely those of the authors and other contributors. These views and opinions do not necessarily represent those of New Book Publishing and Reliance Media Inc.

Table of Contents

1	The Journey Begins	9
2	Immersed in the Word	15
3	The Prayer of Petition	21
4	Prayer at Work	29
5	Leaning on Jesus, One Day at a Time	37
6	Confession Brings Possession	43
7	Trusting Him	47
8	Refresher Course	53
9	God's Word Prevailing	59
10	Believer's Authority	63
11	A Dream Coming to Pass	69
12	God Does Not Send Sickness	73
13	Freedom in Christ	79
14	Having Done All To Stand, Keep Standing	85
15	Do Not Give Up! Grace Will See You Through	89
16	The Body of Christ	97
17	Conclusion	101

This book is dedicated to these very dear people:

Mark

My loving and steadfast husband

Angela, Kimberly, Daniel, and Andrea

The greatest treasures given to me

Faith Family Church

Without you, this book would not have been possible.

Thank you for your love and support.

Foreword

Bev Weirather knows the struggles of attaining healing. Bev's Biblical steps to speaking the right words and standing firm will strengthen and encourage readers as they wait upon God's healing touch in their lives or in the lives of their loved ones.

--Bobbye McNish

*"But to you who fear
My name
The Sun of Righteousness
shall arise
With healing in His wings…"*

Malachi 4:2

Chapter 1:

The Journey Begins

One does not know what a day will bring, but it is a good thing that God does. Nothing takes Him by surprise! However, June 17, 2011, would turn out to be a surprising and shocking day for me, and one that would take me down a road I could not have handled without the Word of God and the help of many people.

I had been experiencing several incidents of pain on my right side, so I made a decision to schedule an appointment at the University of Iowa Hospitals in Iowa City, Iowa, about one hundred miles north of Keokuk, Iowa, my hometown. The gynecology-oncologist on staff was Dr. Amina Ahmed. After an initial CT scan, she diagnosed me with a large reoccurring granulosa cell tumor that was malignant.

I was in total shock at the mention of the "C" word, cancer, as many people are. The tumor was closing off the right ureter, making my right kidney enlarged, so Dr. Ahmed scheduled me to have a stent put in to alleviate the swelling in that kidney. The procedure was unsuccessful, though, because the tumor had grown around the ureter and had blocked the passage.

The next step was to schedule a nephrostomy tube placement for the following day, a procedure I vividly remember, as the medical team could not totally sedate me due to my very low heart rate. They required that I stay the night at the hospital so they could ensure that the tube was working well. I was released the next day to go home and wait for the surgical removal of the tumor which was scheduled for July 11, 2011, the earliest day they could perform the surgery. It would be a three-week wait. Thus began my journey.

Many thoughts spun through my head while I awaited the surgery. I had faith in my God and His promises, but doubtful and fearful thoughts kept hammering away at my mind. I knew, however, that just because I had doubts that provoked me into fear or anxiety, it did not mean I had to give in to them. It is possible, even in the midst of trouble, to control one's thoughts, as **Philippians 4:8** verifies! So, I began to resist those negativities with God's Word in order to get on, and stay on, the path of healing.

Because I had been "tutored" in a church that emphasized the power of what we say, I knew I had to fight the good fight of faith with my words, so I endeavored to speak only God's Word when speaking of the cancer. That is what Jesus did in the wilderness, as recorded in **Matthew 4:1-11**. He spoke scripture in responding to Satan's temptations; therefore, I knew that just thinking on scripture was not enough. The Word needed to come out of my mouth to produce results, just as Jesus had demonstrated, and if HE had to do so, I most definitely had to, also. Jesus is our example of total victory.

I began to search out what God had to say and found some foundational truths. **Isaiah 53:4-5** discloses this: "Surely He has borne our griefs and carried our sorrows; yet we esteemed Him stricken, smitten by God, and afflicted. But He was wounded for our transgressions,

He was bruised for our iniquities; the chastisement for our peace was upon Him, and by His stripes, we are healed."

This scripture refers to Jesus' being whipped thirty-nine times on His back before going to the cross. Through those stripes, He attained our healing. He has already paid the punishment for all our sins and conquered all sickness and disease for us. We do not have to accept them. It became apparent to me that if the scripture said, ". . . by His stripes we *are* healed," (present tense verb,) that healing belonged to me *now*.

There were more scriptures that spoke to me in those weeks before my surgery. "God is not a man that He should lie . . ." according to **Numbers 23:19**. His words are always true, and they will never change, as **Malachi 3:6** states. This is the good news of His Word, and it was very good news to me!

All the things the doctors had told me were just their "facts," and facts can be subject to change. Pain and sickness were "facts" that would leave as I put God's Word into my heart and spoke it out of my mouth. Situations and circumstances would line up with what I believed and spoke. **Romans 4:17** clarifies how to speak God's language by calling those things which do not exist, as though they are. I knew I would have to call for what I wanted, not for what I had, and this would change any bad report I had been given.

The Bible, our instruction manual, declares in **Matthew 12:34**, "For out of the abundance of the heart the mouth speaks." Whatever was in my heart would come out when I spoke. I figured that the number-one way to activate that faith in my heart was to start speaking it.

Many confess how much faith they have, but faith dormant in the hearts of people will do nothing for them. A person must start stirring that faith by speaking healing scriptures into existence. In **Genesis 1**, God spoke the worlds and everything we have into existence. Then, in **Genesis 2**, He made Adam and Eve in His image with the power to speak. I had to use my words to create healing for my body, which is the will of God. He is so good!

In addition, **Mark 11:22-23** is an excellent passage to illustrate the principle of having what we say. Jesus Himself told his disciples, "Have faith in God. For assuredly, I say to you, whoever **says** to this mountain, 'Be removed and be cast into the sea,' and does not doubt in his heart, but believes that those things he **says** will be done, he will have whatever he **says.**" (Boldfacing is mine.) The word "says" is in this scripture three times, so it must be important! (The phrase "this mountain" can refer to any difficult problems we may have.)

Words are the most powerful things in the universe! I cannot emphasize enough the importance of using the right words to create what we desire. "Death and life are in the power of the tongue," states **Proverbs 18:21**. What we say is what we get, and I knew what I wanted to get!

Chapter 2:

Immersed in the Word

Beth Moore, a well-known Bible teacher who ministers to women, said during her study on the Book of Esther, "When we just wait for an *event* (the sale of a home, the birth of a child, a surgery), our strength is depleted, but when we wait upon *the Lord*, our strength is renewed." That was where I found myself during those three weeks before my surgery took place.

I was seeking the Lord, endeavoring to speak the Word, seeking His strength, but I was also human. The pain from the tube in my back was constant. Not only was I being attacked in my body, but I was also still engaging in a constant mind battle through this ordeal. Anxious thoughts would creep in: Am I going to survive? Will I be able to go back to work? How will this affect my children?

I remember a short conversation I had with my wise pastor, Jay Zetterlund, when I was feeling anxious one day. I told him, "I can't heal myself!"

He replied, "No, you can't, and if your husband could heal you, he would." This brief encounter helped me understand, at that exact moment, that no matter how much my husband loved me, ONLY Jesus could manifest His healing power in me, and that was the place to be — in Jesus' loving care.

So, I continued to resist those strength-sapping thoughts which the enemy of God surely wanted me to entertain. In **II Corinthians 10:3-5,** the Word says this: "For though we walk in the flesh, we do not war according to the flesh. For the weapons of our warfare are not carnal, but mighty in God for pulling down strongholds, casting down arguments and every high thing that exalts itself against the knowledge of God, bringing every thought into captivity to the obedience of Christ."

I inherently knew I had to build more faith in my heart. The Amplified Bible describes what faith is in **Hebrews 11:1**, "Now faith is the assurance, (the confirmation, the title deed) of the things [we] hope for, being the proof of things [we] do not see and the conviction of their reality [faith perceiving as real fact what is not revealed to the senses.]"

Romans 10:17 tells us how faith comes: "So then faith comes by hearing and hearing by the Word of God." It is one thing to read healing scriptures once in a while, but it is another thing to read those scriptures on a daily basis to build faith in one's heart. It was essential for me to do this at that point.

What I saw with my eyes and heard with my ears was what I would believe. **Proverbs 4:20-22** was a passage which confirmed that. It declares, "My son, give attention to my words; incline your ear to my sayings. Do not let them depart from your eyes, keep them in the midst of your heart, for they are life to those who find them and **health to all their flesh**." I had to be a doer of the Word, not just a hearer, as Jesus' brother James wrote in **James 1:22.** God's Word was the medicine I desperately needed.

A person who wants to be healed should never take a "faith vacation," or get too busy and neglect to "take this medicine" diligently. Just like I feed my body to stay strong, I had to feed on the written Word of Almighty God to strengthen my spirit. That was how I would acquire faith to receive my healing.

I Corinthians 12:31 says, "But earnestly desire the best gifts." Oral Roberts once said that the best gift is the gift you need at the present time. Mine was healing. Immersing myself in the Bible to build faith (trust in my God) was essential to my healing.

In my preparation time, I watched and listened to many teaching and healing materials. God had miraculously healed Kenneth E. Hagin, at age 17, of a deformed heart and an incurable blood disease. I started re-reading his books: *The Believer's Authority*, *What to Do When Faith Seems Weak & Victory Lost*, his mini book entitled *How to Keep Your Healing,* plus his free magazine, *The Word of Faith*, which was delivered to me monthly. These books caused my faith to come alive!

Kenneth and Gloria Copeland's DVD's from past Believers' Conventions were a major blessing to me as I watched them again. Their daily *Believer's Voice of Victory* television broadcasts and free monthly magazine renewed my trust in God as my healer. Watching Joseph Prince's daily broadcasts liberated me through his teaching about Jesus' grace and its already finished work on the cross, which was my healing.

I digested Keith Moore's CD teaching series called, *God's Will to Heal*. It helped me immensely in understanding why healing is the perfect will of God. After viewing Andrew Wommack's online teaching from 2010, "God Wants You Well," I felt more prepared to stand in faith for my healing.

Another book I had read, prior to my diagnosis, was *The Law of Confession* by Bill Winston. I was so thankful for it because it prepared me to be more conscious of how important my words would be, and how they would change this circumstance. He taught me to boldly speak my faith. If I spoke only what I wanted, not what I had, my healing had to manifest.

Reading a mini-book called *Faith Has No Feelings*, by Norvel Hayes, taught me how to be healed by obeying **James 5:14-15**. One Sunday night at prayer service, in obedience to that scripture, I asked my pastor and the elders of my church to lay hands on me, anointing me with oil.

My sister, Melanie Riley, who has degrees in psychology and social work, was visiting prior to my surgery. She became a huge emotional support to me. Always a great listener and encourager, she soothed my soul as we performed our favorite activity—drinking tea and talking about life. Her clinical perception and inward understanding of who I was helped her to visualize my experiences with fear, faith, and my determination to not give up. A tool to accomplish those behaviors was my faith in God.

In our entire lives together, my sister had only seen me on a few occasions in that much pain and suffering (due to the tube in my back.) We had long talks about how important thoughts were. She believed my faith in God was strong and never doubted I would make it through. We trusted our God to take care of me. All of these avenues contributed to my growing faith and the eventual manifestation of my healing as I waited on the Lord.

Chapter 3:

The Prayer of Petition

My husband Mark had purchased Jerry Savelle's new book, *The Prayer of Petition*. After reading it, I wrote my own petition according to God's eternal Word. I had to break through the impossible and energize my prayer life. (Much of this chapter has been gleaned and paraphrased from Savelle's book, and is being used here by permission.)

If you choose to construct a similar petition, you will need to prepare. Here are the basic steps which you will want to incorporate in writing your own formal request:

- Realize that God is your only source, not others or yourself.
- Trust Him in this process, and know that it is His will for you to be whole.

- Continue studying His Word, and your faith will grow stronger.
- Use your prayer weapons: the name of Jesus, the Word of God, and the Holy Spirit.
- Take time to seek your Healer, and prepare your heart before you construct the petition.
- Remember, God's Word is the final authority. Let His Word and the Holy Spirit guide you to specific scriptures to write. (The Lord quickened several verses for me to use in the formal request I prepared.)
- Write your request, and use it as a point of contact to release your faith to receive what you have asked for. This earnest request is clear-cut and definite. **Matthew 21:22** states, "And whatever things you ask in prayer, believing, you will receive."

Jerry Savelle says that thanksgiving is a vital part of this petition. Read your constructed petition out loud to God, and thank Him for hearing your request and healing you. This helps you to remember that God is the one who makes it all possible. Count it done in the spiritual realm, remembering your covenant with Him. Then, stop worrying and start praising God for doing exactly what you asked Him to do.

Reach out to others by praying for them to be healed. Show confidence that God has heard your request and is performing His Word, as **Jeremiah 1:12** mentions. Let the peace of God keep you focused as you guard your thoughts. Be prepared to stand your ground and not give up when the enemy's lies surround you. God, who is the Creator of the universe, is faithful to His Word. Never blame God when it looks as though nothing is working. The problem is not with God, but with our lack of determining to stand forever.

Above all, confess His love for you. Remind yourself that everything He has accomplished has been for *you*. Use my petition, which follows, as a sample for yourself if you choose. (For full instructions on how to write the prayer of petition, please refer to Jerry Savelle's book, *Prayer of Petition*.)

Here is the petition I wrote to my Heavenly Father:

*Be it known, on June 26, 2011, at 6:45 P.M., that I receive the healing of my body. I have obeyed Your Word in **James 5:14-15** that says this: "Is anyone among you sick? Let him call for the elders of the church and let them pray over him, anointing him with oil in the name of the Lord, and the prayer of faith shall save the sick, and the Lord shall raise him up, and if he has committed sins, he will be forgiven."*

*I stand on Your Word and allow it to heal me from the top of my head to the soles of my feet. Also, according to **Luke 1:37**, "For with God, nothing will be impossible." So, this circumstance is not impossible with You, Lord. As I stand on the Word of God and declare it, it will make possibilities out of impossibilities!*

*Your Word declares in **II Timothy 1:7**,*

"God has not given us a spirit of fear, but of power and of love and of a sound mind," so I reject any fearful thoughts coming to my mind as I stand on that Word.

*I humble myself, therefore, under the mighty hand of God, that He may exalt me in due time, casting all my care upon Him, for He cares for me, as **I Peter 5:6-7** says I should do.*

*You declared in **III John: 2**, by the apostle Paul, "Beloved, I pray that you may prosper in all things and be in health, just as your soul prospers." So, I know it is Your will for me to be well from this sickness and disease.*

*Throughout **Psalm 136**, Your servant David said, "Your mercy endures forever." **Hosea 6:6** also states, "For I desire mercy and not sacrifice." So, I want to thank you, Heavenly Father, for having healing mercy on me right now.*

Thank you for redeeming me from the

*curse of the law as **Galatians 3:13** states, because Jesus became a curse for me. It is written in Your holy Word, "Cursed is everyone who hangs on a tree," (referring to Jesus) so that by my receiving Christ Jesus, the blessing promised to Abraham will come upon me. I receive that redemption now by the blood of Jesus.*

Praise You, holy God, merciful God, wonderful loving God, and precious Jesus for healing me of this cancerous tumor, and I thank You eternally for making me whole and helping me to walk in divine health forevermore! Praise Your HOLY NAME FOREVER! AMEN! So be it!

-Bev Weirather

I consistently read the prayer of petition and declared that I had received the healing of my body on June 26, 2011, by faith, because of obedience to His Word. When I chose to walk by faith, I believed that I had healing *now*.

Psalm 23:4 comforted me in this challenging time. It says, "Yea, though I walk through the valley of the shadow of death, I will fear no evil; for You are with me. Your rod and Your staff, they comfort me." Shadows never hurt anyone. I would walk out of this valley of death and into the healing promise of God!

Chapter 4:

Prayer at Work

July 11, 2011, the day of surgery, finally arrived. I was Dr. Ahmed's last patient of the day. She did not anticipate any problems, went over a few preliminaries, and then I was taken to the operating room. The next thing I remember was groggily waking up in the ICU Ward the following day.

Dr. Ahmed came in, took my hand, and told me, "The surgery was not as successful as I had anticipated because I could not remove the tumor. It was a very strange flat tumor," she said. (Looking back, I recall my pastor cursing that tumor in the name of Jesus and commanding it to die, to shrink up, and to leave my body. I believe that in the three weeks of waiting on surgery, the tumor had started to do just that—the possible explanation of its being flat.) My doctor went on to say that the tumor was attached to my tailbone, and that I could have bled to death if she had proceeded.

When I heard this very disturbing news, I distinctly remember asking Dr. Ahmed, "Why did you not try to remove the tumor and let me bleed to death and go on home to be with Jesus?" I felt it would have been easier to have departed to be with Christ in Heaven (**Philippians 1:23**) at that point.

Her loving response, as she held my hand within her own skillful hands was, "Oh no, I could not do that!" What a good doctor she was to help save my life. My emotions had been talking.

Later, I heard more details from my sister, Joleen Nachbar, the Nursing Supervisor at Kansas City Cancer Center, who was spokesperson for my family at the time. She had contacted the Iowa City hospital the day after surgery to see how I was, because she had not heard and was very concerned. A nurse connected Joleen with my doctor for the details of what had transpired.

Dr. Ahmed told her that she had tried to cut part of

the tumor out, but because it was so vascular (supplied with many blood vessels), she could not proceed to remove any more of it, or I would have died due to blood loss, and she had to save my life. It had been a perilous surgery. I had experienced lung failure due to losing huge amounts of blood, and the medical team had to replace the blood as fast as they could do so, via transfusion through my right carotid artery. In addition, lymph nodes were removed on the right side.

Joleen later relayed to my family that Dr. Ahmed was very mentally and emotionally exhausted after the surgery. It had taken a very huge toll on her that day, and she felt devastated due to almost losing me as a patient. However, through the doctor's very competent hands and, I believe, through the prayers of others, angels were sent out to watch over me, and I stayed alive.

I found out later that many Christian people were praying for me from everywhere. One of my own daughters, Angela, had an amazing experience in prayer the day I was in surgery. Here it is in her words:

> *On the day of my mother's surgery, I was*

praying fervently for her. At one point, I felt I was done praying, in the sense that I had asked my Father for something, and I believed that He had ALREADY done it, so, instead of continuing in prayer, I was praising my Father for the victory. I knew my mother would live — He had told me she would! However, in the middle of rejoicing, the Holy Spirit suddenly stopped me and said, "Pray in the Spirit for your mother."

I answered, wondering if it was a test, "Nope! I already prayed, and I know (smiling the whole time) that by Jesus' stripes my mother is completely whole!" Again, the Spirit spoke, this time with urgency, and even though I didn't understand why He would have me asking for something that I knew He had already given me, I obeyed.

I got on my knees, and after a half hour or so, I saw, in the Spirit, thick beams of light emanating from me, from the south, and from the northeast; there were smaller beams coming from many other directions as well, but they all joined into one as they moved just north of me. I knew the beam of light was headed to Iowa City where my mom was in surgery, and I also knew immediately that it was the power of the Holy Spirit honoring the prayers of the righteous.

As the vision faded, joy filled my soul, and I began singing and dancing. I laughed and cried because I knew that my Father was trustworthy of taking total care of my mother. I had such peace.

It would be two to three weeks before I found out that she had almost died on that operating table. She had lost what I understood to be a vast amount of blood, yet she lived! I know for a fact that it was the Lord honoring the prayer of His people that kept my mother alive during that surgery. He is so faithful!

--Angela Wise

Thank you, Angie, for being obedient to the Holy Spirit's prompting and for being the cherished prayer warrior that your mother needed! I truly believe it *was* prayer that kept me alive. Otherwise, I would be in Heaven today. In Jesse Duplantis' personal testimony of going to Heaven in 1988, *Close Encounters of the God Kind,* he reveals how wonderful Heaven is! This recording on DVD tells about all the beauty and glory of our eternal home where we will go someday.

Yes, I will go to Heaven because I gave my heart to Jesus many years ago, but I will not go until I am fully satisfied, and at a full age, as in **Job 5:26**! As my pastor stated, "You are not going to Heaven yet. You have many more things to accomplish here on the earth, and your work is not done."

I am thankful to everyone who was obedient to the Lord and prayed for me! There were many, I am sure. My pastor's mother Deanna was told by the Spirit to pray specifically against the spirit of death, and she obeyed. Pastor Jay Zetterlund was also praying fervently. Moreover, his son Adam, who was living in Paris at the time, was led by the Spirit to pray for me the day of my surgery, even though he was completely unaware of what was going on. It is amazing how God works through His people when they are obedient!

Leaving the ICU ward after a day and a half, I was transferred to a regular room for a few days. They tried to get me up to walk again, but the cutting of blood vessels from the tumor, plus the surgery, affected my right leg muscles. They were incapable of working properly. Several units of potassium were administered through my right carotid artery. (Because I had lost so much blood, my heart rhythm was affected.)

Although I was not expecting to need all this care, later I was very thankful for the superb medical team that assisted me. At the end of the week, I made a decision to go home. Even though I was very weak, tired, and in pain, I thought home was a better place to be, so my husband Mark drove me there.

Chapter 5:

Leaning on Jesus, One Day at a Time

Now at home, I would start recovering. My daughters, Angela, Kimberly, and Andrea, each helped in their own ways: cleaning my home, praying for me, running errands, picking up necessary medications, visiting me on a frequent basis, and doing whatever I needed. I was very grateful for them!

My son Daniel could not visit me, but he sent many encouraging letters to let me know he was praying for me, reminded me how strong I really was, and said that everything would be fine. In one letter, he told me only to speak and believe what I wanted and to stay in the Word, which was exactly what I intended to do. Thank you, Danny! Your heartfelt words were a beacon of light to me in my dark moments!

Moreover, I was grateful to my sons-in-law, Joe Wise and Mike Settles, for graciously and generously giving their wives (my daughters) the freedom to assist me during this time. Of course, seeing my five grandsons, Drake, Zane, Brayden, Payton, and Caleb, was a source of great happiness, too!

My brother, Rick Gray, who also lives in Keokuk, brightened many of my days by his presence. He brought me a beautiful chrysanthemum on my birthday in August, and we visited. During the next few months, he stopped by to check on how I was doing and to see if there was anything he could do. He has always been a super big brother watching over me! All conversations we had were about his concerns for me, and how he genuinely wanted me well. I so appreciate his love and concern!

Many members of my church family, too numerous to name here, showed kindness in various ways by bringing meals, baking cookies, continuing to pray for me, and assisting in any way they could. They used their gifts to help me recover quickly. You know who you are. Thank you so much for letting Christ use you to bless me in my time of need! Truly, it is appreciated!

One dear friend, Leeanne Humiston, the nursing instructor at Southeastern Community College, was called a time or two for her expertise when I did not know what to do next. She insisted that I take my medications, brought delicious food, and nursed me until I was better. Moreover, I listened to great praise music on the MP3 player that she brought, and so my spirit and soul were nurtured as well. Leeanne was marvelous at taking care of me in my worst moments and was a beautiful example of the compassion of Christ!

Another cherished friend and co-worker, Bobbye McNish, who is a strong believer in the Lord, called me frequently, prayed daily for me, and stopped by when I was feeling up to a visit. She brought Mark and me dinner a time or two and helped until I was able to stand long enough to cook. Mostly, she was there for me spiritually, always believing and confirming to me that I *was* the healed of the Lord. I knew I could count on her for anything, including loving me right where I was. What a tremendous blessing close friends are!

Howard and Lisa Pappenfus, very close church friends who had moved with their triplets back home to Minnesota several years ago, made arrangements to come in August of 2011 just to take care of me after my surgery and to do chores I could not do. They stayed four days to assist Mark and me physically and emotionally. In addition, their 13-year-old triplets prayed for me every day, and for that I was so very grateful. Thank you, Paige, Blair, and Luke!

In addition, Susan Kerr, another precious friend, also kept in touch with me on a regular basis, brought small gifts to cheer me, and never gave up on the belief that I would be made whole. Always having my best interests at heart, she gently encouraged me to follow up with the second round of radiation. Her promise to take me to her childhood home out East after all of this was over gave me something joyful to anticipate. Good friends are great treasures!

I must include my husband Mark here. He was with me the whole time and helped me immensely. He never left my side in the hospital and did not return to work for a week. Even when he did go back to work, he would call or text to check up on me. I could not have recovered so quickly if he had not taken such good care of me and allowed me to rest. At that point, I had to depend on him to do most everything for me. He was a real trooper!

After a few weeks, I started to feel better, although it was a slower process than I had surmised. My sister Joleen was able to come for a visit a few weeks later. She has been a nurse for thirty-two years and was able to give me some tender loving care and necessary medical guidance. Her advice was, "You've been through a lot, Bev. You don't have to be brave. Rest and take your medications." I had been told that before, and, finally, I decided to obey the repeated instructions. Her medical counsel, gentleness, and kindness were invaluable to me in those difficult days recovering from so many issues!

Prayer and medicine can go hand-in-hand. God created us a three-part being: spirit, soul, and body. God deals with us in all three realms, and when our body is shouting, we need to give it some relief and not feel guilty for doing so. We must not allow pride to talk us into being foolish and presumptuous by assuming we do not need the medical field's assistance.

When I was again able to do so, I started to confess the Word of God on a daily basis, and to thank Him for healing me. Sometimes, when I was awake in the midnight hours, I expressed my thanks that the Holy Spirit was, and is, my Supreme Helper. As soon as I felt well enough to walk, I returned to church and heard the Word being preached. I kept saying that God would restore health to me and heal me of all my wounds, as **Jeremiah 30:17** promises. I was so thankful to be alive!

Chapter 6:

Confession Brings Possession

By August, I was actually dancing a little while listening to a Rhema Singers & Band song called, "Healer in the House." Four weeks earlier I had felt I would never be able to do that again, but I did. The power of God was in my body effecting a healing and a cure. There was a healer at work in my house, and His name was Jesus.

As the song was playing, an interesting thing happened. God reminded me of the day I got married to Mark. After the ceremony, I had made a fist and said, "Yes!" symbolizing victory. It was a confession (a word of faith coming from my mouth) and a prayer come true. God showed me that all the confessions I had made for months about having a godly husband brought about that marriage.

In the same way, my healing confessions would bring about wholeness in my body. He told me that my wedding day was a celebration of what I had already received by faith many months before. The day I got married was *not* the day I received my husband; it was just the manifestation of my prayers and confessions. He continued to tell me, "Just like that situation came to pass, so will your healing as you confess my Word and believe it."

As time went on, I was reminded to pray in the Spirit (in other tongues) more often because the Holy Spirit knows all things. Terri Copeland Pearsons calls it "God's Swiss Army knife" because it has many tools: gifts of the Spirit, wisdom, revealing, and mysteries unlocked. Praying in the Spirit is praying the perfect will of God out of *our* spirits, instead of praying with our head knowledge, which is limited.

While in the presence of Jesus one day, He told me, "Quit being angry at yourself for not being well, and just receive My mercy and healing." Blaming myself and analyzing *why* I was sick was not helping me. In fact, when I started down the path of doing that, I was getting precariously close to siding with the "accuser of the brethren" (Satan) who loves to make us feel guilty **(Revelation 12:10).**

Jesus, however, perceiving my thoughts, came to my rescue. Whether the sickness was partially of my own doing, whether it came from just living life on this planet, or whether it was a direct attack of the enemy, Jesus still wanted me to call on Him so my health would be restored, as He happily desired. He was, is, and always will be our Deliverer and Restorer. He makes all things new.

On his daily broadcast, Joseph Prince was consistently preaching, "Grace, grace, grace! It is finished!" I did not have to feel guilty or do one more thing to be healed. It was already an accomplished fact. I just needed to receive it and declare the already purchased work of Calvary as **I Peter 2:24** states.

God is not going to send Jesus back to be beaten again for our healing. It was done over two thousand years ago. The sinless, spotless Son of God was the perfect sacrifice for our sins, paying the price for all our wrongdoing so we would not have to! Glory to God!

Praise His holy name forever!

God was so gentle in leading me by His Holy Spirit and showing me what to do, what *not* to do, and what to say to attain victory. His wisdom is there for the asking. He is, was, and always will be **El Shaddai**—God Almighty—who is more than enough to demolish any mountain that stands in our way!

Chapter 7:

Trusting Him

In late August, the time had come to begin the radiation treatments that Dr. Ahmed had recommended. God informs us of His purposes in **Psalm 73:24**, "You (God) will guide me with Your counsel." I questioned the Lord about having the treatments, and I believe He told me yes, to go forward. In a conversation He had with me about this subject, He told me that this sickness was not unto death, but that God would be glorified by my healing, as Jesus says in **John 11:4**. My daughter Angela said God had revealed the same to her at an earlier time. It was great to have this confirmed by my Savior.

However, on my way to the radiation treatments at Great River Medical Center in Burlington, Iowa, I had to travel through Fort Madison, Iowa, every day. I would pass by a cemetery there, and the devil would tell me, "You had better get your affairs in order, because you will be gone in three months."

Waves of fear would come over me. However, **James 4:7** tells us to resist the devil, and he will flee. So, I resisted those thoughts by declaring, "You're a liar, devil!" and the fear would leave.

I John 4:18 tells us this: "There is no fear in love; but perfect love casts out fear, because fear involves torment." Fear comes straight from the pit of Hell itself, trying to persuade a person that there is no way out. It has to be dealt with through speaking healing scriptures, or a feeling of helplessness will follow. When we resist Satan in the name of Jesus, he has to desist in his maneuvers!

One particular day when I was not feeling my best, and happened to be traveling alone to my radiation treatment, I was just bombarded with defeating thoughts. The Holy Spirit jogged my memory and reminded me that I had recently received one of Keith Moore's free quarterly CD's called, "Trusting Him." I swiftly slipped it into my truck's CD player and listened. Keith was saying,

"Go into trust mode." He spoke of **Psalm 91:16** that says, "With long life I (God) will satisfy him and show him My salvation."

As Keith expounded on this scripture, I began to confess aloud what he was saying: "No matter what is coming against me, I cannot perish. I have not run my race; I have not finished my course. So, I cannot die with this stupid disease."

He went on to say that if people keep it just that simple, just believing God's Word, they will live and prevail. Miracles will happen to them, and they will come out! He encouraged me, as he always has, to trust in the Lord with all my heart no matter what I felt or thought. Speaking those words helped me to stay in faith and to do just that—to trust Him. Thank you to one of my favorite teachers in the Body of Christ, Brother Keith Moore!

While undergoing the daily radiation treatments at Great River Cancer Care Center, I was cared for immensely by the staff there. My nurse, Deb Grogan, had much compassion on me as days went into weeks, and I became very sick and weak. She took extra time answering questions and giving solutions to many problems I was experiencing. Also, Peggy Link, the receptionist, who had been a cancer patient there previously, understood first-hand what I was experiencing. She was very kind and compassionate to me on the days when I checked in but was not feeling well. Her many suggestions eased my pain and my heavy heart. Both of these women were Christians and prayed for me.

However, after only fifteen of the recommended twenty-five treatments of radiation, the doctor stopped them. I became so ill I could not eat and lost a significant amount of weight. I became very weak and dehydrated. The doctor said it was rare to be sick so soon, but because of the location of the tumor, perhaps my bowel had been affected by the radiation. If the dehydration continued, they would admit me to the hospital.

Being confined to home was not what I had expected! However, **Psalm 91:2** expressed my intention to combat these severe symptoms: "I will say of the Lord, 'He is my refuge and my fortress; my God, in Him I will trust.'" Listening to Keith Moore's music CD, *The Peace of God*, which is full of Bible scriptures, significantly aided me in trusting God's promises. The songs flooded my soul with peace, which was what I absolutely needed to stay focused on my healing journey.

During this time, my kind and giving mother, Marlene Gray, visited as often as possible. However, because she herself was recovering from surgery, she was not able to assist me with physical things as much as she really wanted, which made her feel rather helpless. The desire of her heart, though, was to help, and that she did! She would cover my hand with her loving one and tell me sincerely, "I pray for you every day, every night. I know you will get well." She would tell me to rest, and then she would slip out. Her words were sweetness and nourishment to my soul!

I had to hold fast to my profession of faith in this time of weakness. As **Hebrews 4:15** tells us, "For we do not have a High Priest who cannot sympathize with our weaknesses, but was in all points tempted as we are, yet without sin." Jesus is touched with the feelings of our infirmities and weaknesses, but He is moved by

FAITH alone. Harassing thoughts pummeled my mind. However, I had the sword of the Spirit, which is the Word of God, to fight the battle waged against me, as referred to in **Ephesians 6:17.** Resting frequently and taking my medications helped with the discomforts, while I kept confessing, "I trust you God."

Chapter 8:

Refresher Course

In the third week of September, I attended a Dr. Ed Dufresne conference in Cedar Rapids, Iowa, at Spirit of Faith Family Church. I had been impressed by the Holy Spirit to attend. While there, I basically encountered a refresher course on healing. Several people spoke into my life, which was a confirmation of what a friend of mine, Pam Hamilton, had spoken to me earlier that Thursday. Having always been a great friend and cheerleader in my life, she spoke words of encouragement on the phone. She believed God was going to reveal some things to me that I needed to hear that night at the meeting.

Pam was right! One of the ladies from the praise and worship team walked over to me and told me to continue to praise God for my victory, because like Kenneth E. Hagin always said, "The praise cure works." If I believed I was healed, I needed to praise God that it was already done. It was already mine!

She also talked about forgiveness. I quickly responded, "I am quick to forgive others." She said that she was not finished yet. I sheepishly said, "Ok." Then, she started to share about how we need to forgive *ourselves*, which started me crying. It spoke volumes to my heart! I cried because I believe God was speaking through that lady in order to get me into a forgiving mode so I could receive. It was a tender moment when I knew how much my Father God must love me to speak through a perfect stranger and to help me realize He already had forgiven me for everything.

Nothing could stop me from being healed—not any of my past sins. They were gone by the blood of Christ. It was not about my being perfect, but about His love, mercy, and forgiveness. Sometimes we do forgive others, but find it hard to forgive ourselves. However, it is very necessary to do that so we can receive all of God's goodness. God never withholds anything good from us, but we can have trouble receiving His blessings by not only being unforgiving towards others, but also towards ourselves.

Another lady (who sat next to me) told me her testimony of being freed from anxiety and fear attacks. I realized my need to repent—change direction—for allowing fear into my life, which can sometimes keep the door to sickness open. In fact, allowing fear into our lives is distrusting our Father to take care of us. The Holy Spirit spoke to my heart and told me to do three things: Think right, speak right and treat people right.

Before another one of the meetings, I knew I needed to purchase a book by Dr. Dufresne's wife Nancy. It is called *A Sound Disciplined Mind*. Her book was straight to the point and reminded me to be on the offense in speaking to the fears that were coming to me daily. Another one of Nancy's articles, "How to Keep Your Healing," talks about the enemy: "The devil has been eternally defeated, but he has yet to be imprisoned; therefore, we must fight the fight of faith."

What does that mean? It means that I need to continually say what God's Word says about my healing, regardless of what thoughts the enemy might try to tell my mind, and regardless of what symptoms I might notice in my body. No matter how I feel, I am still to believe that Jesus purchased my healing; therefore, I am healed NOW!

Jesus declares in **John 10:10** that we have an enemy who comes to steal, kill, and destroy. We are told in **Revelation 3:11**, ". . . hold fast what you have . . . ." so the enemy cannot steal it. We need to speak the Word of God to counter his insidious attacks. When we do, we shut him down, stay in faith, and, instead, receive from God all His goodness.

This reminded me of an eye-opening statement I had once heard Pastor Creflo Dollar declare when he mentioned that a person cannot fight a thought with a thought. In Chapter 6 of his book, *Eight Steps to Create the Life You Want,* he states, "You must become a vigilant custodian over your thought life and allow the Word of God to be the guardian of your mind." It is so true! Our mouth is our weapon against Satan's lying accusations. We need to speak back to those evil thoughts in order to be victorious.

On the last night of the meetings, Dr. Dufresne taught on **Matthew 8:17**. The scripture states, ". . . He Himself (talking about Jesus) took our infirmities and bore our sicknesses." That means He relieved us of them and carried them away from us. We do not have them.

Dr. Dufresne followed up with a demonstration of that concept. He had all who needed healing write their diseases and sicknesses on index cards. After that, he taped the cards to a gentleman who was representing Jesus. This man then walked out of the sanctuary with those index cards pinned on him. It was as clear as a bell to me after witnessing that object lesson: Jesus *took* my sickness, and I did not have to bear it anymore!

At the end of the meeting, I was ready to stand in the healing line for Dr. Dufresne to lay hands on me. The ushers helped us get in line, but they directed me to the left, not to the right where Dr. Dufresne was ministering. I was prayed for by another minister named Johnny. Directly after praying for me, he said emphatically, "It's over!"

I took that word by faith. I believed I had received another anointing that breaks the yoke. God had shown me that even though Dr. Ed Dufresne was anointed by the Lord to heal cancer, he was just a vessel. We are not to go looking to a man, but to Jesus. That is why I believe God had another minister lay hands on me.

God did NOT do things the way I thought He would or should, but He was teaching me a very valuable lesson. I actually walked back to my seat dumbfounded. Later, I was able to laugh at how God does things that go past our minds but register in our spirits. God knows what to do, and what will work for each person. I was refreshed from the meetings, was learning how to keep my healing, and was very determined and encouraged after that day to stay the course.

Chapter 9:

God's Word Prevailing

When I returned to Dr. Ahmed's office in Iowa City the following Friday, October 7, 2011, another CT scan showed the tumor had shrunk to half its size. I told her that it must have been more prayer than radiation, because the radiation oncologist in Burlington had discussed it with me, and he firmly believed that the three weeks of treatment would not be very effective.

Dr. Ahmed was happy and very pleasantly surprised about the fact that it was shrinking, but she wanted to see it gone. However, I was very reluctant to go back for more radiation and to experience more severe symptoms. A decision had to be made within a week, or it would be too late to receive any more treatments. (Radiation is designed to be a continuous process. Therefore, it had to be done within a certain time frame to achieve maximum results.)

Following a week of struggling with the issue, I called my wonderful pastor, and we had a long talk. The decision to finish the radiation was made because I had to know in my heart that I had done everything in my power to get better in the natural. Like Pastor Jay told me, "It is not medicine *or* faith. We can use both."

I had to agree with him. There had been a time in my life when I thought my faith was weak if I needed a physician's care. (In fact, in some cases, people will NOT get proper medical attention just to prove how spiritual they are.) However, the lack of pursuing professional medical help does not make someone more spiritual! So, Pastor Jay prayed for me, and together we agreed, through faith in Jesus' name, that the symptoms would not be as severe.

With my decision made, the radiation oncologist scheduled me for another twelve rounds of treatments. They were more tolerable than the first doses of radiation, and I kept reminding myself of what the Holy Spirit had shown me before the treatments began: One day while sitting in my living room, I had been directed by Him to look down at one of my beverage coasters which a very sweet friend, Linda Buckert, had given me in August for my birthday. The scripture quotation on it, **Psalm 91:11**, from the English Standard Version of the Bible, said, "For He will command His angels concerning you, to guard you in all your ways."

To me, that meant the angels of God would protect me while going through the treatments. God's Word in **Psalm 46:1-2** was working: "God is our refuge and strength, a very present help in trouble. Therefore, we will not fear. . . ." My omniscient God was guiding and comforting me with the exact scripture I needed at that very moment!

My church was still standing with me for victory throughout all the treatments and procedures. Every Sunday night at the prayer service, whether I was able to attend or not, they would continue to thank God for my total healing.

Moreover, my perceptive pastor would, on occasion, pray individually just for Mark. He knew that Mark had a need for prayer and support, too. Sometimes spouses can be overlooked, unintentionally, because the main focus is on the one who needs healing. However, husbands and wives are one, so when one hurts the other hurts, also. I can never thank my pastor and church enough for their thoughtfulness and selflessness. Without them, I shudder to think what would have happened to me.

Each day it seemed I was being helped by God through so many believers, and I do not take that for granted. I believe that when I get to Heaven, I will have the revelation of how many people were involved in this process of healing. Yes, He definitely had the plan. It was the will of God for me to be well, but it was not automatic like some people think. Nothing this side of heaven gets done unless people first find out what the will of God is, and then pray to God for what they need. The people who prayed for me knew that, and would not accept anything but God's best for me.

Chapter 10:

Believer's Authority

On November 18, 2011, I went back to Iowa City for another procedure to rid me of the tube in my right kidney. It was not successful, and I was left in a great deal of pain for two full days. My good friend, Jeanne Riney, reminded me that Billye Brim Ministries had live healing services every third week on their website, so on November 20, I watched the service.

David Horton, whom I had never seen before, was preaching. He kept going over the fact that in **II Corinthians 5:17** the Word declares, "Therefore, if anyone is in Christ, he is a new creation; old things have passed away; behold, all things have become new." Verse 19 of the same chapter says, ". . . God was in Christ, reconciling the world to Himself, not imputing their trespasses to them and has committed to us the word of reconciliation."

Colossians 1:13 says, "He has delivered us from the power of darkness and conveyed us into the kingdom of the Son of His love." Jesus has already defeated Satan. Satan can only try to deceive us into believing he has power to hurt us. He has no real power!

As I mentioned earlier, our greatest battle is the battle of our thoughts. If we are ever going to be victorious, we need to think God's thoughts about ourselves. God is not mad at us! He has taken care of all the sin problems the world will ever know. We need to align our thoughts with God's thoughts, the Bible, and then declare who we really are. **II Corinthians 5:21** says, "For He made Him who knew no sin to be sin for us, that we might become the righteousness of God in Him."

We have right standing with God *now* because of what Christ did for us, not only on the cross, but also in hell as He defeated the devil and ransomed us back to our Father. Jesus says in **John 17:23**, ". . . and that the world may know that You have sent Me, and have loved them as You have loved Me." God loves us as much as He loves Jesus! When He sees us, He sees us covered by the precious redeeming blood of Jesus. Is that not amazing!

God is not withholding anything from us. We do not have to wait until we are perfect for God to show us His goodness, heal us, or provide for us. It is by grace, His gift, that we are healed. We need to learn how to simply go to our "Abba Father," and receive what we require. (*Abba* is an Aramaic word meaning "father," and it has the connotation of being an endearing term, such as when a child trustingly says, "Daddy.")

After watching the Billye Brim service, I was again encouraged. God knew exactly what I needed to hear. However, the next day I started to experience a terrible headache, which is very unusual for me, and by the following day, I was starting to feel worse, with chills and a fever. It dawned on me that the devil was trying to put flu symptoms on my already hurting body.

I told God, "I need to get a breakthrough!" Sometimes we just get plain tired and worn out feeling bad! Remembering what David Horton had spoken, I got furious with the devil. I spoke and said, "I take authority over you in the name of Jesus. Take your lying symptoms and go back to hell with them because I am not going to have the flu!" After a little while, the chills left and the fever broke. I was starting to feel dramatically better.

We know this from Jesus' own words in **John 8:44:** ". . . he (Satan) is a liar and the father of it." He is forever bringing falsehoods to our minds, but we have authority over him through Jesus. We need to stop listening to him and boldly declare **Psalm 107:2**. It tells us, "Let the redeemed of the Lord say so." We *are* the redeemed of the Lord and need to be saying, "I am redeemed!"

That night, I was reading an article called, "A Fresh Spark," by Kenneth Copeland, which appeared in his December 2011 issue of the *Believer's Voice of Victory*. It, too, was exactly what I needed to hear. The Holy Spirit was helping me realize that whether we are lay people or preachers, we all have problems and issues. God wants to help us, but He needs to have something to work with, namely our words of faith. We also need to be thankful, even while we are hurting, and know that as we stand on His healing promises, He will perform them on our behalf.

I Thessalonians 5:18 says, "In everything give thanks; for this is the will of God in Christ Jesus for you." I did not need to be thankful *for* the circumstance, but did need to be thankful *in* it. Because people get weary, this is not always easy. However, if we are consistently thankful for what is good in our lives, we will walk in the light, the pain will eventually have to leave, and the body will heal. As Kenneth Copeland's wife Gloria says, "In consistency lies the power." We must be consistent in our confessions.

At the Wednesday night communion service before Thanksgiving, I was again feeling great and giving God praise for His healing power at work in my body. (It was at this exact communion service when the Holy Spirit instructed me to start journaling my road to recovery so that others could be strengthened and have hope that their lives could change, also.)

In **Matthew 6:33**, Jesus profoundly exclaims, "But seek first the kingdom of God and His righteousness, and all these things shall be added to you." The presence of God is what we need to seek. If we seek the giver, instead of the gifts, we will be doubly blessed. One minute in the presence of God, as He reveals His love and mercy to us, is better than anything this world can offer. What a great Father He has been to me!

Chapter 11:

A Dream Coming to Pass

A few days later, after all the Thanksgiving company had gone, I fell asleep on the couch. Suddenly, I woke up and knew I had experienced a "God dream." I have had only a few of these dreams, but I knew immediately it was God revealing something to me.

In the dream, a female doctor, dressed in a white coat, kept pointing to a blank sheet of paper. She would look up at me, look at the paper and point, then look up at me again, but she was saying nothing. At first, I did not comprehend what she was trying to convey, but, finally, I understood it. There was *NOTHING THERE*! The paper was blank, which meant to me, NO TUMOR! So, I started declaring, "The tumor is gone! Nothing is impossible with God!"

Six days later, I was scheduled to be in Iowa City for another CT scan. We awoke early the day of the appointment, and, as always, Mark drove me there so that I could focus my thoughts on the positive and not be distracted in any way. I could always depend on him to be steady and sure, which was not easy for me to do on those trips to the hospital. He always made me feel safe, secure, and comfortable, and was Jesus in the flesh to me in those moments. Taking care of me was not easy, but Mark was always compliant with my pleas for help.

We arrived, and another CT scan was administered. When the results came in, Dr. Ahmed relayed the wonderful news to me. The tumor, indeed, was completely gone! There was a grey area where it had previously been located, but she could not find any tumor! As we sat there pondering the good news, Mark and I praised God softly. I looked over at him, saw his smiling face, and felt the joy in his heart. The dream had come true! **GLORY BE TO GOD!**

While Mark drove us home, I texted the awesome news to my pastor's wife Shannon and also to my family and friends. Everyone was rejoicing with me! People were crying while they texted or called me. It brought great joy to all who heard the news! I had always told God that I would give *ONLY HIM* the glory for such a marvelous healing manifestation. **GLORY TO YOU, LORD!**

It had been an extremely exciting but long day at the hospital, and when I finally arrived home, I needed to rest. As I lay down, a thought promptly came to me (from Satan) that I was so unworthy to be healed. He was trying to inject thoughts into my mind, hoping I would repeat them with my mouth, so he could have the authority to steal my healing.

Immediately, I heard a strong warning in my spirit from the Lord, *"Don't say that! I paid a horrible price for you to be healed!"* I knew it was the Spirit of God helping me to stop a counter-attack from the enemy. If the devil could not keep me from getting healed, he would try to steal it from me by bringing thoughts that were contrary to the will of God, or by giving me lying symptoms. I rebuked them. Satan is a liar—the father of lies. It is his nature to send deception from the pit of hell, and as Nancy Dufresne says, those lies of the enemy deserve no recognition.

It was celebration time indeed! Mark thought it would be nice to celebrate our victory by going out to eat at a local restaurant that night. Although I was not very hungry, we went and enjoyed a relaxed dinner. We were both very relieved after the wonderful news we had heard that morning. God had been so faithful to us both, and we were then, and always will be, very thankful for His healing power extended towards me. God is good all the time!

Chapter 12:

God Does Not Send Sickness

The next day, while meeting some of my friends for lunch, I shared my testimony with an acquaintance who also happened to be there. I was very excited as I explained to her how God had healed me. One of her very sincere comments was, "God must have had some purpose in allowing this cancer, though."

I replied to this person, "God is not the author of sickness and disease. The only evil purpose for this sickness was to steal my life, and it came from Satan, not God. Jesus makes it plain in **John 10:10** what is really happening: 'The thief does not come except to steal and to kill and to destroy.'"

Many people have been inaccurately taught that

everything that happens is God's will, so let me be clear: God is good, the devil is evil. Until truth is known, it is hard to have faith. Kenneth E. Hagin clarified this concept by saying he believed that faith begins where the will of God is known.

The Bible is very clear in describing sickness and disease and its origin. In **Job 2:7**, the Bible says that the devil made Job sick. **Psalm 41:8** says that disease is evil. In **Luke 13:16**, Jesus Himself calls sickness satanic bondage. Peter states in **Acts 10:38** that sickness is satanic oppression. When we embrace the truth of God's Word, we get healed, because the truth sets us free. God is *not* the destroyer, but Jehovah-Rapha, the God who still heals!

A misconception that prevails in the minds of some people is wondering if it is God's *will* to heal them. To ascertain the will of God, let us look to Jesus, who is the express will of the Father in action. In **Mark 1:40-42** a leper came to Jesus and said, "If You are willing, You can make me clean."

"Then Jesus, moved with compassion, stretched out His hand and touched him, and said to him, 'I am willing;

be cleansed.' As soon as He had spoken, immediately the leprosy left him, and he was cleansed." This confirmation in scripture reveals that it is God's will for people to be healed.

Another misconception is that it is not His will to heal *everyone*. The Bible tells us differently in **Luke 4:40**: ". . . all those who had any that were sick with various diseases brought them to Him, and He laid His hands on every one of them and healed them." God has never changed His mind concerning healing, and wants all people well. Not once did anyone come to Jesus in faith and not get his or her healing.

One more misconception is that many believe God has put the sickness on them to teach them something. Thus, they stay sick. However, according to **I Corinthians 2:13,** the Holy Spirit is our teacher, not sickness. God is a good and all-wise Father, and He is love. Consider this: Would loving earthly parents expose their child to a debilitating illness on purpose? Of course not! Would they break the child's arm in order to teach him or her a lesson? No! That would be absurd, and very illegal! Neither does

God send sickness to His children to teach them a lesson.

Jesus said this in **Matthew 7:9-11:** "Which of you, if his son asks for bread, will give him a stone? Or if he asks for a fish, will give him a snake? If you, then, though you are evil, know how to give good gifts to your children, how much more will your Father in heaven give good gifts to those who ask Him!" (NIV Bible) God is good, and the giver of good.

In his book, *How to Walk in the Supernatural Power of God*, Guillermo Maldonado says, "Some think that sickness is a punishment sent by God, or that their suffering brings glory to God. Others use the Bible to try to justify their illnesses. None of these things are scripturally correct." Later, Maldonado adds, "According to Scripture, the power of sickness was destroyed by Christ over two thousand years ago. If this is so, why are people still getting sick? In truth, sickness expired the day Jesus paid the price for our iniquities on the cross of Calvary. Therefore, it is illegal for sickness to enter the bodies of believers. Healing is not a divine gift; it is a legal right."

My pastor, Jay Zetterlund, who has an amazing

teaching gift, said this about the origin of sickness: "Too often there have been religious reasons given for why sickness happens, but, ultimately, the perfect world that our God created has been subjected to the curse of an enemy for generations." He went on to say, "Whether it is the direct hand of demonic activity that makes us sick or simply living life on a planet that is still very much under his dark influence, Satan is the ultimate source of those things that 'steal, kill, and destroy.' He has perverted life into death, and no matter how long we live, death still seems so very unnatural . . . because God has always planned for us to live eternally."

Nevertheless, there are people who will say that they grew so close to God during their illness, that so much good came out of their illness, and that they learned so much during it, that it *must* have been God's will for them to go through it. The people who say this are usually very sincere and probably love God. However, they should consider this: *God is so skilled at turning bad things for our good, that He often gets blamed for sending the bad thing in the first place!* **Romans 8:28** says, "And we know that in all things God works for the good of those who love him. . . ." (NIV Bible) Thank you, God, for bringing good out of what was meant for our harm!

Finally, many people do not have knowledge of God's will for them to be healed; therefore, they are deceived by that lack and accept beliefs that do not line up with the Bible. **Hosea 4:6** states this: "My people are destroyed for lack of knowledge . . . ." Satan is the source of powerless, defeated beliefs. God would be unjust to allow Jesus to bear all our sins, sicknesses, and pains (**Isaiah 53:4**), and then expect us to carry them again. Thank God that He is just!

Chapter 13:

Freedom in Christ

Although the tumor was gone, I still had the nephrostomy tube in my right kidney. The Interventional Radiology Department at the University of Iowa Hospitals had tried in November of 2011 to place another stent, and that, too, had been unsuccessful. At that point, my only option was to have another major surgery, which Dr. Ahmed said she *could* do but did not want to because I was not healed from the first surgery yet, and an additional operation would involve more scar tissue. I could not imagine going through another major surgery!

In February of 2012, I returned to the hospital and was told they would examine the ureter again, but probably would not retry the stent. They found that the tumor and/or radiation had caused one-third of the lower right ureter to become ninety percent blocked and severely scarred. Mark and I came home very disappointed after the second failed attempt to rid me of the need for the tube in my kidney.

However, Mark thought of a doctor who might be able to help us, and he called him that night. This doctor recommended scheduling an appointment with a colleague who was a "straight-shooter" who would give us the truth, so we did that.

My new urologist in Fort Madison was Dr. Louie Kantzavalos, better known as Dr. Louie. At our initial visit, he said that it would be a major surgery to reconstruct the ureter to rid me of the tube. He would not attempt it, but would send me to Mayo Clinic in Rochester, Minnesota, but only if the procedure he had in mind showed that the ureter was not working properly.

So, he scheduled another trip to outpatient surgery in order to take a look at the problem. After the procedure, he said he would not want to try a stent either because it was too torturous. However, he shot dye up to the kidney, and the dye came back down through the ureter, which indicated my kidney and ureter were functioning, at least partially. He did not see why we could not work towards getting the tube capped and removed, if possible. When he connected with my team of doctors in Iowa City, they made a plan for the permanent removal of the tube.

At the next trip to Intervention Radiology in Iowa City, on April 16, 2012, I had the tube changed (a procedure that was done every two months), and cultures were taken. Nine days later, I went back to Dr. Louie, and he said that after antibiotics and some tests, we would be able to see where we were.

The next week, I had more renal scans and ultrasounds showing that the kidney was draining, just more slowly than the left one. Dr. Louie asked if I wanted to cap it off and see how it went. I said, "Yes!" So, he capped off the tube and then scheduled another ultrasound. Two days later he came into the room at the clinic and gave me a high-five. He told me all looked good!

The tube came out permanently on May 9, 2012. I was so excited to be free from that extremely annoying and very painful part of my life which had been there for almost a year, and I was (and am) so very grateful to Dr. Louie!

By faith I kept confessing that my kidneys were working properly, and that my ureter was opening up. What had been an impossible thing from one doctor's standpoint became a reality through another doctor's decision to take a risk. On August 15, 2012, I went for a three-month follow-up, and Dr. Louie said my kidneys were doing great, blood work was good, and there was no infection! He said that he would see me in nine months, and when I returned for a checkup in June of 2013, everything still looked good!

Back on July 6, 2012, I had also followed up in Iowa City with Dr. Ahmed for another CT scan. She said the CT scan was stable, and there was no tumor. Taking this opportunity to convey my sincere thanks to her for helping me stay alive, I let her know I was very grateful for having such a great surgeon. She humbly smiled. Pointing up to Heaven, to recognize God's hand in all of this and to give Him the ultimate glory for healing me, I said to her, "But He healed me." She nodded her head in agreement.

Hearing that the kidney tube removal had been

successful made my doctor very happy. She told me how beautiful she thought I looked that day, which was quite a testimony to the healing power of God. A year earlier, she had seen the frail, weak person I had become after surgery, a person who could not walk without aid to an appointment. Another follow-up CT scan on April 19, 2013, showed the same good news! No tumor! **All the Glory goes to God!**

Chapter 14:

Having Done All to Stand, Keep Standing

Two years have come and gone since I was first diagnosed with an inoperable tumor. After recovering for over a year, I decided to return to work, even though there were still some minor symptoms I had to deal with from the radiation and surgical procedures. Persistently, I used (and still use) my faith by speaking to my body parts and commanding them to come into line with the word of God.

Psalm 34:19 encouraged me in these times. It says, "Many are the afflictions of the righteous, but the Lord delivers him out of them all." According to the Bible, I am the righteousness of God in Christ; therefore, God would continue to deliver me out of *all* my afflictions.

Romans 8:11 says, "But if the Spirit of Him who

raised Jesus from the dead dwells in you, He who raised Christ from the dead, will also give life to your mortal bodies through His Spirit who dwells in you." Numerous times, Pastor Jay would encourage me with this exact scripture. By the leading of the Holy Spirit, he knew what I needed to hear. Thank God for good pastors!

The same power of the Holy Spirit that caused that tumor to leave my body is still at work bringing about a healing and a cure for other parts of my body that need to function properly, as God originally intended. There is *life* in the Word of God as it is spoken and believed.

Even if people have some damaged body parts like I have had, God can give them a new part. According to Gary Wood, God has a spare-parts room for those who need a miracle. In 1966, Gary died in a car accident, left his body, and went to Heaven. While there, he was shown a spare-parts room with every kind of body part a person would ever need.

Gary went on to say that if people would only believe, and not doubt while asking the Father for the body parts they need, the angels would be on their way to dispense them. However, if a person spoke doubt and unbelief, it would stop the angels in delivering the body parts. After his sister prayed for him, Gary returned to his body, recovered, and shared his experience with others in his book entitled, *A Place Called Heaven*.

II Corinthians 1:20 says, "For all the promises of God in Him are Yes, and in Him Amen (so be it), to the glory of God through us." It glorifies God when we believe His promise of healing. God has promised it to us in His never-changing Word. In His infinite love and kindness, He has provided for all of His children in every way possible to receive whatever they need in this life. **Jeremiah 32:27** tells us, "Behold, I am the Lord, the God of all flesh. Is there anything too hard for Me?" No, nothing is too hard for our King of Kings and Lord of Lords!

Chapter 15:

Do Not Give Up! Grace Will See You Through

I have endeavored to be as truthful, factual, and genuine as possible in sharing the events of my journey to healing. It is very important that one understands this was not an easy journey! It did not come to me overnight, but was a process. It would have been phenomenal to have been miraculously healed in an instant, but it did not happen that way for me. It did happen in time, though. Regardless of the time factor, one must trust God in the journey to healing. People requiring healing need to know that even if it is slow in coming, they should NOT GIVE UP. IT IS ON ITS WAY!

Yes, the victory comes in never giving up no matter how long it takes. We do not play nine-inning games, we play until we win, as I have heard Kenneth Copeland say many times. **Romans 5:17** inspires us when it says, "For if by one man's offense death reigned through the one (Adam), much more those who receive abundance of grace and of the gift of righteousness will reign in life through the One, Jesus Christ." We are created to rule and reign in this life over any obstacle in our path. We win every time we remain steadfast in our believing and speaking.

Furthermore, God expects us to walk in the light of what we know about healing. I positively believe that I did do that at the beginning of my journey, and I did what I could do in the natural to get well, too. For example, I did some juicing to get my body toxic-free so it could heal more efficiently, because cancer *is* toxic. Also, a friend recommended I drink Essiac Tea while doing radiation. He said it is reputed to be very beneficial for those who cannot have surgical removal of a tumor. Moreover, I ate raw apricot seeds, also reputed to kill cancer cells due to the vitamin B-17 in them. (I am not a doctor, and do not make claims that these natural things will help people, and am not suggesting that they do the same. I am just mentioning a few things I tried.)

There is something I *can* claim with assurance, however, and it is this: There is only One who has perfect knowledge of all things. His name is Jesus, and I trusted Him to do what only He could do in the supernatural to make me well. **Job 12:13** says, "With Him (God) are wisdom and strength, He has counsel and understanding." Ultimately, the main healing came from my God. I could not do just the natural things to get well—I had to believe the Word.

Even though I am a woman of God, I am a human being first. I needed to change and grow more into the image of God daily. For example, there were times when I would get angry because I was hurting, and I would say fearful or doubting words. I was not as spiritual as I wanted to be some days, and I had to ask people to please bear with me and keep praying for me, because I was (and am) no different from anyone else. I asked God for mercy and grace, and He extended it.

When I started this journey, I did not understand what true grace was. His grace (unmerited favor) was unveiled to me moment by moment, through the Spirit of God. This revelation brought me to the end of myself and connected me with the person of grace, Jesus, in a most intimate way. I learned I could not depend on my own self-efforts, but that I had to depend completely on the unmerited favor and blessings of God. It changed my attitudes, thoughts, and actions.

The healing of my body was my main focus at the beginning of this journey. Little did I know that my soul (which is my mind, will, and emotions) would also be restored. I highly recommend the book, *Unmerited Favor*, by Joseph Prince. It radically changed my thinking in many areas that needed to be transformed. As he states in Chapter 17, "Right living is the result of right believing." He goes on to say, "Christianity is not about behavior modification. It is about inward heart transformation." How true!

Furthermore, Joseph Prince tells us in his book that Jesus is interested in our total well-being, and He can mend any part of us as we look to Him to be our only answer to every aspect of our lives. It is not about us and our efforts, but about His grace and favor. His grace will energize us, revive us, heal us, and bring us out of our devastation into God's marvelous light where there is no darkness. As **I John 1:5** explains, ". . . God is light and in Him is no darkness at all." This is the place where every part of us gets whole.

I do not claim to be a teacher in the body of Christ, but there is One who is, and that is the Holy Spirit who can teach us and guide us through our healing—spirit, soul and body. Jesus states in **John 16:13**, "However, when He, the Spirit of truth, has come, He will guide you into all truth; for He will not speak on His own authority, but whatever He hears, He will speak; and He will tell you things to come." Please allow the Spirit of God, who knows all things, to gently guide you through to victory on your journey.

In the Amplified Bible, we read in **II Peter 1:2**, "May grace (God's favor) and peace (which is perfect well-being, all necessary good, all spiritual prosperity, and freedom from fears and agitating passions and moral conflicts) be multiplied to you in [the full, personal, precise, and correct] knowledge of God and of Jesus our Lord." God's unmerited favor (His grace) will increase in our lives as we gain more knowledge of our Savior Jesus Christ and His finished work at the cross, which is our inheritance. This will cause us to enjoy success beyond our natural ability, intelligence, or qualifications.

Realize that God does not show partiality in His grace, as Peter stated in **Acts 10:34.** Paul also gave us that revelation in **Romans 2:11**, and **Ephesians 6:9**. These repetitive truths from God's Word reveal God's nature and our position with Him.

To find out God's will, we look to Jesus, because He is the express image of God. The Bible says in **Acts 10:38**, "how God anointed Jesus of Nazareth with the Holy Spirit and with power, who went about doing good and healing all who were oppressed by the devil, for God was with Him." God loves us all the same, and His will is for *all* to be healed. He does not show favoritism by healing some and not others.

Jesus never failed to heal people unless they were full of unbelief, as **Matthew 13:58** states: "Now He did not do many mighty works there because of their unbelief." It was not that Jesus *would not* heal; it was that He *could not* because of their unbelief. People who come to Him can receive whatever they need if they only believe that He will. Grace brought me through, and it will do the same for you!

We all go through storms in this life which will test our faith to see what we really believe. I encounter many people who are facing storms of sickness in their own lives and need a miracle. If it happens in an instant, glory to God! However, if it does not, keep your faith in God's Word, which is the power to heal you. Remember, His grace can overcome anything arrayed against you. He will never fail you!

All people need encouragement from others when they are in challenging positions. I pray that I have done just that for you in this book, for that is my motive. **As Psalm 136** states over and over, "For His mercy endures forever." He was merciful to me every day, right where I was, and He will do the same for you!

Chapter 16:

The Body of Christ

After she read my journal, my pastor's wife, Shannon Zetterlund, encouraged me to create a book which would help others who needed healing. If she had not used her huge gift of exhortation, this book would not be a reality. I appreciate her boldness and sincere honesty very much. Thank you, Shannon!

There were many people in churches other than my own who were lifting me to the Father through prayer. I want to thank them, also, for their part in helping me achieve this healing. It was not a "lone ranger" effort, and I recognize that wholeheartedly. God loves to use His Body, the church, when we need help.

I Corinthians 12:20 states, "But now, indeed, there are many members, yet one body." The theme of this chapter is to recognize that all the members are necessary. It is unnecessary for us to walk in pride, thinking we have to fight the battle on our own. That is the devil's plan. He likes to keep us isolated, but we need to depend on others to aid us in our time of need, especially those who are of the household of faith, our Christian brothers and sisters.

It is paramount that I include my husband Mark here. He went above and beyond his duties to make sure I was comfortable, taken care of, and well-rested. Mark not only worked two jobs while I could not work, but was available when I needed him, which was a daily necessity. **Ephesians 5:25** instructs husbands to love their wives, "just as Christ also loved the church and gave Himself for her." Thank you, Mark, for being that godly husband and for caring for me as Christ cares for His Body, the church. I cannot begin to thank you enough for all the selfless hours, days, weeks, and months you invested into my welfare. You are a vast treasure to me!

In addition, I am eternally grateful that Mark, my mother, and Shannon spoke into my life every chance they got saying, "I *know* you are healed." It helped me remember His faithfulness. No matter how spiritual we think we are, we need others to encourage us and to remind us how faithful our Father in Heaven really is.

It is appropriate for me to acknowledge two other people who helped me immensely. My daughter Kim helped in a huge way with all the technological aspects of getting this book ready for print. Her vast knowledge of computers was a great source of peacefulness to my mind. She guided me step by step in getting documents completed, sent, and authorized by the publishing company. Thank you, Kim, for sharing your wealth of knowledge to help make this a smooth process. You are a rare gem!

Also, I want to thank my good friend, Andrea Crooks, for editing this book from beginning to end. Being an English teacher for most of thirty-five years, she was very competent to critique the content, to cause it to flow together, and to help polish the book so that the reader would understand my heart and intent. I so appreciate her many hours of volunteer work that went into helping create my book. Andrea, you are a true blessing in my life!

Finally, for everyone who had a part in my healing

process, I thank you from the bottom of my heart, and so does Jesus. If I do not know your name, you know who you are. Someday when I get to Heaven, I will personally come up to you, hold your hand in mine, and thank you.

Chapter 17:

Conclusion

So there you have it, my journey to healing. There are never enough words to convey what I felt during this journey. I love to talk, but I was almost speechless when the manifestation of healing took place. Even though I was speaking my faith and believing for healing, when it came, I had difficulty articulating what was happening in my heart. It was so sacred and worthy of worship.

I am ever so thankful to my Lord and Savior Jesus Christ for making all this come to pass. Because of His selfless sacrifice more than two thousand years ago at the cross, I am now well on my way to wholeness—spirit, soul, and body.

Ephesians 3:20-21 is so real to me: "Now to Him who is able to do exceedingly, abundantly, above all that we ask or think, according to the power that works in us, to Him be glory in the church by Christ Jesus to all generations, forever and ever. Amen." His great love has made possible all things that I believed, and it is more than I could have imagined!

Let me encourage you with these final words: If you do not know Jesus as your Lord and Savior, you can this very moment. He loves you more than anyone could ever love you on this earth. He proved it by laying down His life for you, stretching forth His arms, and hanging on the cross just for you! Jesus said in **John 14:6,** "I am the way, the truth, and the life. No one comes to the Father except through Me." He is the *only* bridge to the Father and the *only way to eternal life* as **John 3:15** exclaims.

Knowing Jesus is a simple prayer away. Right now, say this with your mouth, and mean it in your heart: *"Lord Jesus, come into my heart. Forgive me of my sins. I do believe that You are the Son of God, that You died in my place, and that You were raised from the dead so that I can live forever with You. Fill me with the Holy Spirit. Amen!"* It is done! Ask and receive. It is that simple. Then, start thanking Him for saving you. Welcome to the family of God!

Find a church to attend that believes the whole Bible so your faith can grow strong as you connect with other Christian believers. Study the scriptures in **bold** print I have included in this book. They have the power to strengthen you and to set you free. Then, go help someone else discover the good news of the gospel that you have just heard!

***TO HIM BE ALL THE GLORY
FOREVER AND EVER! AMEN!***

***GOD'S WORD WORKS!
SPEAK IT AND DECLARE IT
IN THE MIDST
OF YOUR STORM,
AND WATCH
FOR GOD'S RESULTS!
BE HEALED
IN HIS WONDERFUL NAME!***

About the Author

Bev(Gray)Weirather was born in Quincy, Illinois, and grew up in Hamilton, Illinois. She relocated to Keokuk, Iowa, in 1976. After watching Billy Graham on television in the summer of 1973, she gave her life to the Lord and became a born-again Christian. In 1989, she began attending Agape Fellowship Church in Keokuk, Iowa. The church later changed its name to Faith Family Church. It was in this church that she grew up spiritually and was introduced to some of the greatest ministries in the world. Their teachings changed her life and were crucial in her development as a Christian.

Bev has worked in the children's ministry at Faith Family Church for over twenty years.

She has enjoyed visiting the elderly in nursing and convalescent centers and leading many residents to the Lord.

Bev believes that she has the call of evangelism on her life—the call to lead unbelievers to Jesus. As a United States Postal Worker (USPS), Bev had the opportunity to meet many people one-on-one and to share the love of God with them. She was able to pray for those who had a need from God and witnessed the power of God at work in their lives.

In 2004, Bev became a licensed minister for Jail Ministry for Jesus. She has been privileged to preach and teach at a local county jail and at a local detention center, and she has seen many men and women come to the saving grace that only Jesus provides.

After working for the USPS for twenty years, Bev made a career change and began working for the Keokuk Community School District as a licensed para-educator. She continues to encourage others daily with her heart of compassion.

Bev has three daughters: Angela Wise, Kimberly Settles, and Andrea Weirather, and one son, Daniel Ringstrom. Bev married Mark Weirather in September of 1994. She and her husband reside in Keokuk, Iowa.

Need additional copies?

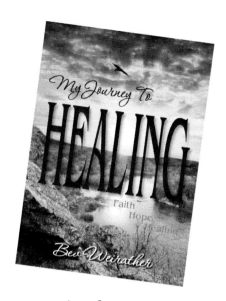

To order more copies of

My Journey To HEALING

contact NewBookPublishing.com

- ❐ Order online at

  NewBookPublishing.com/Bookstore

- ❐ Call 877-311-5100 or

- ❐ Email Info@NewBookPublishing.com